Snails

Susanna Davidson

Illustrated by
Rocío Martínez

Reading Consultant: Alison Kelly
Roehampton University

In a sunny garden,

inside
flower pots

and under
rocks,

lots of snails
are hiding.

3

The snails wait until
it is dark.

Then they creep out.

Snails have soft bodies and hard shells.

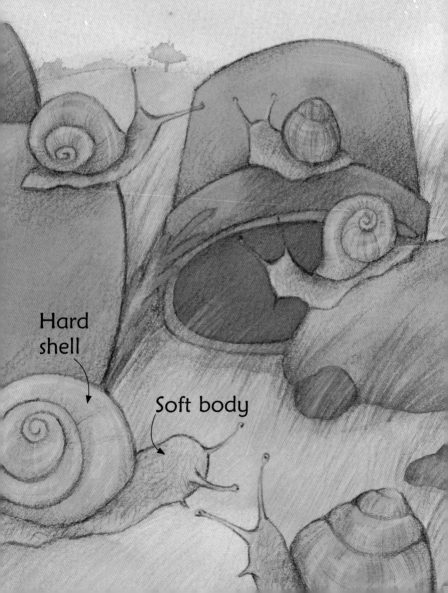

Hard shell

Soft body

Slime oozes out from
under a snail's body.

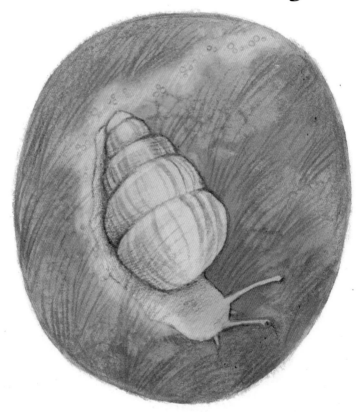

It helps snails slide
over the ground...

up branches...

...and even
upside down.

Hungry snails look for food.

They have rough tongues.

They rub their tongues
over leaves to eat them.

Snails feel their way
around with feelers.

Feeler

Feeler   Feelers

They can smell with
their feelers, too.

10

Their eyes are on the
ends of the longer feelers.

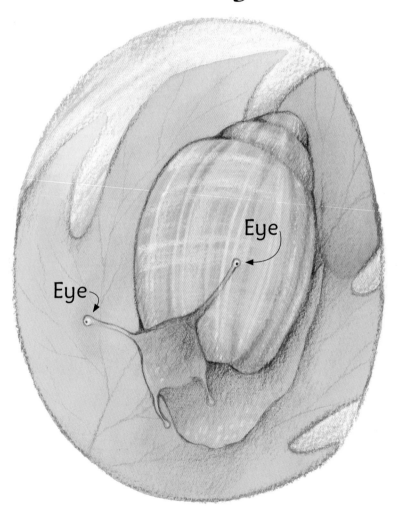

Eye

Eye

A bird swoops down.
It is looking for food.

The snails hide in
their shells.

The bird can't get
them. It flies away.

Some kinds of snails
live in ponds.

And some kinds live in the sea.

Some snails are huge.

They can grow longer
than your arm.

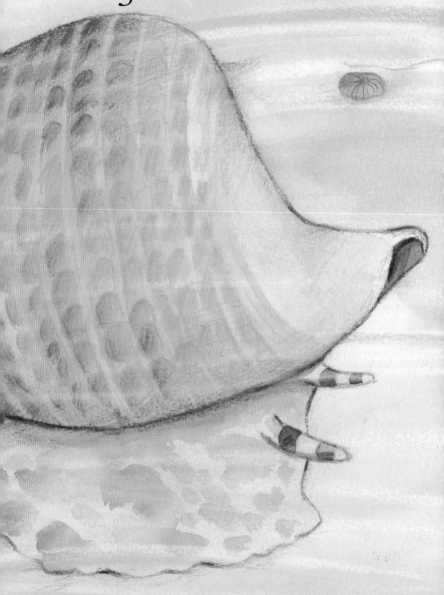

Snails lay lots and lots
of eggs.

On land, snails lay their
eggs in the ground.

A baby snail is inside each egg.

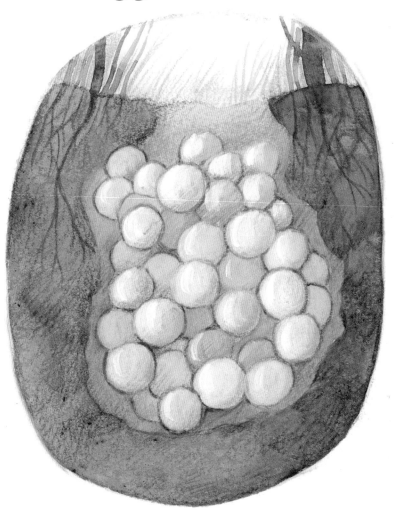

Pond snails lay sticky
eggs on plants.

Their eggs are inside
blobs of jelly.

This keeps
them safe.

After a few weeks, the
baby snails hatch out.

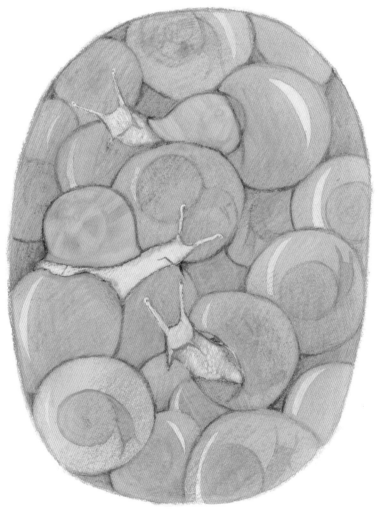

They eat

and eat

and eat.

The snails' bodies grow
– and so do their shells.

23

It's easy to find snails.

Just follow their
slimy trails.

25

Snail facts

 The biggest land snails
live in Africa. They can grow
to 38cm (15 inches) long.

 Snails go to sleep
in winter and wake up
again in the spring.

Snails come out after rain because they like the wet.

The bottom of a snail's body is called its foot.

Some birds can eat snails. They smash the shells on stones.

PUZZLES

Puzzle 1
Can you match the words
to the different parts of
the snail?

shell

foot

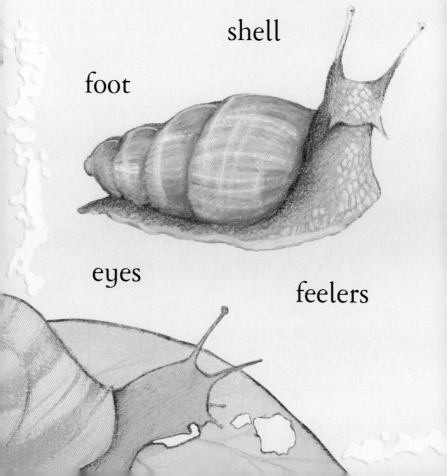

eyes

feelers

Puzzle 2
Can you see...

- one bird
- two butterflies
- six snails

Answers to puzzles

Puzzle 1

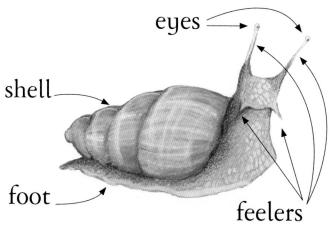

eyes

shell

foot

feelers

Puzzle 2

- one bird
- two butterflies
- six snails

Index

Snail websites

You can find out more about snails
by going to the Usborne Quicklinks
Website www.usborne-quicklinks.com
and typing in the keywords "first
reading snails". Then click on the link
for the website you want to visit.

Internet Guidelines
The recommended websites are regularly reviewed
and updated but, please note, Usborne Publishing is
not responsible for the content of any website other
than its own. We recommend that young children
are supervised while on the internet.

Zoological consultant: Dr. George McGavin
Designed by Maria Pearson
Additional design by Louise Flutter
Series editor: Lesley Sims
Series designer: Russell Punter

First published in 2008 by Usborne Publishing Ltd.,
Usborne House, 83-85 Saffron Hill, London EC1N 8RT, England.
www.usborne.com Copyright © 2008 Usborne Publishing Ltd.